Creating A New You in Six Weeks

Dr. Rosie Milligan

Milligan Books   **California**

Copyright © 2002 By Dr. Rosie Milligan
Los Angeles, California
All rights reserved
Printed and Bound in the United States of America

Published and Distributed by:
Milligan Books
an imprint of Professional Business Consultants
1425 W. Manchester, Suite C
Los Angeles, California 90047
(323) 750-3592

Typeset by
Jo Ann Johnson

Formatting by
Alpha Desktop Publishing

First Printing January 2002
10 9 8 7 6 5 4 3 2

ISBN 1-881524-69-8

TABLE OF CONTENTS

TABLE OF CONTENTS

DEDICATION

This book is dedicated to Ms. Linda Clemons, the fabulous host of the Saturday morning talk show, "Sister Talk"

This book is also dedicated to the Sister-Friends who participated in the "Six Weeks To A New You" class, via Linda's radio talk show, and especially the woman in her 50's, who was motivated to enroll in nursing school after completing the class. We applaud you for pursuing the vocation that you have wanted for a very long time.

ABOUT THE AUTHOR

Dr. Rosie Milligan

Dr. Rosie Milligan, registered nurse, counselor/health consultant, author, and Ph.D. in Business Administration, has always been an achiever. Every career or business she's been involved in has included helping other people accomplish what they wanted in life. Her motto, "Erase 'NO,' Step Over 'CAN'T,' and Move Forward With Life," has been a motivating influence for hundreds to whom she has been mentor and role model.

The mother of three entrepreneurs—an M.D., a cosmetologist, and a health food store owner—Dr. Milligan lectures nationally on economic empowerment, managing diversity in the workplace, and male/female relationships. Her books, **"Starting a Business Made Simple" and "Getting Out of Debt Made Simple"** have helped many across the country. She is the author of ten other books.

As an economic empowerment activist, the Mississippi native owns a bookstore and Professional Business Consulting Services—providing consultation for new and small businesses and staff development training for corporations. In 1998, she started a

6

publishing company, Milligan Books, where she has published over 100 new African-American authors in the past three years. Her publishing company is the fastest growing publishing company owned by a female in the nation.

A successful motivational speaker and trainer, she has appeared on numerous television and radio shows, such as Sally Jesse Raphael in New York; A.M. Philadelphia; Evening Exchange in Washington, D.C., Marilyn Kagan Show in Los Angeles, and she's a regular guest on Stevie Wonder's KJLH Radio. She is founder and director of "**Black Writers on Tour,**" and a columnist for "**Black Issue Book Review Magazine.**"

Dr. Milligan is obviously a woman who knows no limits and has proven this with her newest venture, Milligan Literary Agency. She recently sold her first work, *The Shirt Off His Back,* to one of the largest and most prestigious publishing houses.

INTRODUCTION

It is my intention to encourage people to live their dreams and to embrace change, without fears and concerns about what others may think and feel.

I am not saying do not consider others in your quest for happiness. I am saying, consider yourself first. You must consider "balance" when your choices impact the lives of your family. However, you should seek purpose for your existence.

I conducted a workshop in early 1990 called "Erase No." During this workshop, we conducted an exercise called "Dream Your Dreams." We played soft meditation music. We asked the participants to close their eyes and listen to the facilitator. The facilitator spoke the following words softly, as the participants, with eyes closed, listened.

"If you were in control of your life, what would you be doing right now? Would you be working in the profession that you are now in? Are you happy doing what you do? Are you on your own agenda or someone else's?"

The facilitator stopped the music and asked the participants to open their eyes. There were only a few dry eyes in the room. I then asked volunteers to share with the group what they were feeling and the reason for the tears during the exercise.

Most of them admitted that they were unhappy. They had jobs but no dreams. Many stated that they were more moved by the question, "Are you on your own agenda?" The following are quotes from the participants:

"I am a teacher because my family are teachers. They wanted me to not break the cycle."

"My father wanted me to be a doctor because he did not have the opportunity. I wanted to make my dad happy. Medicine is one way of making good money."

"I am not in love with sports. However, playing ball did afford me a college education. I like the prestige now and the money, but really I am not as happy as I could be and I would rather do something else."

This seminar motivated me to seek ways to assist people in making life changes and to seek personal happiness, without feeling guilty, when they disappoint family and friends. You can never give what you do not possess. If you do not have joy and happiness, you cannot give it to your family. You are responsible for your own happiness. You can only make others happy when you are happy. If you need a new prescription for life, you must embrace change. You are never too old and it is never too late to change. You can have all the joy and happiness you desire if you are willing to just change.

Your first exercise will be
Your dream list

When we think of the word dream, what comes to mind is something we hope for—something we want—something we see ourselves having or doing. We have practiced this dream list with groups for years. The participants are excited as they perform the exercise where money is no object. Their demeanor changes drastically, when they begin to perform the dream list exercise where money is an object.

Our observation has been that most people change their mind regarding what they want to have and do, based on their present financial status. The purpose of this dream exercise is two-fold:

•• Help people to understand the importance of having dreams.

•• Help people to see that their ability to dream big should not be predicated on their current bank balance.

The bottom line is that your present financial status should not prohibit you from dreaming and thinking big. So get back to thinking big and having dreams.

It is time for you to do your dream list. Your first list is where money is no object. Your second dream list is where money is an object.

ON YOUR MARK, READY, SET, GO!

(Play soft instrumental music as you perform this exercise.)

DREAM LIST

"MONEY IS NO OBJECT"

Things I want to have or do within the next year:

I WANT	NAME THE MONTH YOU WANT IT.

Things I want to have or do within the next two years:

I WANT	NAME THE MONTH YOU WANT IT.

DREAM LIST

"MONEY IS AN OBJECT"

Things I want to have or do within the next year:

I WANT	NAME THE MONTH YOU WANT IT.

Things I want to have or do within the next two years:

I WANT	NAME THE MONTH YOU WANT IT.

GOAL SETTING

People need to seek balance when goal setting. During our many empowerment workshops, we observed that most participants expressed goals that were financially dependent, such as:

- To purchase a large home for my family
- To open my own business
- To open a home for girls, boys, the elderly, etc.
- To buy a new car
- To put my children in private school

While most people are firm on their financial goals, many will not obtain them due to shortsightedness. For those persons who believe that lack of money is what stands in the way of their achieving their goals, they will more than likely fail.

There are many areas in our lives that we need to improve on and to set goals for, in order to reach our full potential. Below is a list of areas that may be underdeveloped in your life that may serve as a blockage to reaching your financial goals.

Personal —

    How you truly feel about yourself, your self-worth, and what you believe you should have in this life.

14

Mental —

Your attitude, your motivating drive, and willingness to take charge of your destiny.

Family —

Your relationship with your family, your ability to balance your career and family life.

Spiritual —

Your belief in God. Your inner peace and your source of strength.

Career —

How you feel about the work you do. Your accomplishments and your relationships with the people you work for.

Social —

Do you have good social skills? Are you a net-worker?

Physical —

Do you feel good about your physical appearance? Are you in good health? How is your energy level?

Sexual —

Are you satisfied with your sexuality?

It is crucial for you to complete the exercises and worksheets throughout this manual. It is also imperative that you assess these areas in your life. These exercises will help you to take a close-up look at yourself. They serve as a mirror and also a reminder, along the way, of the progress you have made and the changes you need to make.

WEEK ONE

Personal – Things that are for you only

It is a time for all things. And it is definitely a time to be self-centered and feel good about it.

You should not feel guilty when you take time to do for yourself while excluding others.

Learn how to say no and not feel guilty. When someone asks you, "Can you do me a favor, or can you help me do something today, etc, etc.?" have them be specific about what they are requesting from you before you answer. Saying Yes to everyone leaves you feeling tired, overworked and worn-out.

When you take a close-up look at the things you do for others and the things you do for yourself on a daily basis, you will be shocked at how much you don't do for yourself.

Learn to be alone and not feel lonely. Learn to enjoy spending time with self. Experience dining alone—go to the movies alone—visit a play alone. You will soon discover that other people are a luxury and not a necessity.

It's Now Time to:

- Make a change
- Create a new attitude
- Say out loud it's my turn

So stop feeling guilty during your shopping spree, and celebrate the beginning of your new journey, creating a new you.

WEEK ONE

Mental – developing a mindset that is conducive to good mental health, and balancing your emotions.

Making changes creates a battlefield in the mind. Two opposing forces are in operation. One force wants to experience a new way of life, while the other force wants to play it safe and remain in its comfort zone.

This is a good time to inventory your mental status. Ask yourself a few questions. Yes, have a conversation with self, and answer self, and no, you are not going crazy, you are seeking sanity and balance.

Stand in front of the mirror and ask your mind this question, "Hey, mind, what's up, where you at?" As you listen to the response, observe to see if your facial expressions match the response.

Your mental status holds the key to your success. Therefore it is vital to examine how you view self.

For all that we can imagine doing, and all that we do or not do, is a direct result of that picture that we have for "self." And that picture is derived from our total experiences—from birth until now. However, the images that we have for ourselves are often based upon how others see us through their own perceptual lens.

Ask yourself a few questions.

- Am I happy, if not why?
- Am I unhappy, if so why?
- Is my state of happiness or unhappiness based on what I feel about myself or what others feel about me?
- Am I a people pleaser or do I seek to please myself?
- Do I take responsibility for the unhappiness of others?
- Can someone other than myself make me happy?
- Ultimately who is responsible for my happiness?

Your first week of excursion is a perfect time to take a look at your attitude. As the old adage says, "Your attitude determines your altitude."

Are you on your way?
or
Are you in your way?

Take a close-up look at your attitude about life and all its perplexities.

> *Life is not a bed of roses*
> *and*
> *Neither is life a bed of thrones*

Do you have a positive attitude about yourself as well as the world around you? I believe that our external view is a direct reflection of our internal personal view.

> *What you think about your world*
> *determines*
> *what you think about the world*

Food for the attitude

> *The neighbors' clothes on the*
> *line may be cleaner than you*
> *think if you would wash your*
> *windows before looking out of them*

While one woman complained that the young people would not give up their seat, another woman, standing, saw her bus ride as an excursion and a chance to really get to see the city.

While one man raved and cursed for two hours about some one cutting his car tire, another man, thanked God that he stopped the Devil from cutting the other three. He fixed the tire and was up and rolling in ten minutes.

Week one is very critical to the success of your new journey. How you view self, and your mental status, will determine the time that it will take for you to create the new you that you deserve to be.

Guard and protect your mind. It is your personal computer. You should protect your mind from the Virus bug.

ON YOUR MARK, READY, SET, GO!

1. Study your Goal Setting Scale. page 24

2. Turn to your worksheet called Goal Setting Work-sheet. page 25

3. Complete the Goal Setting Worksheet for all items of concern from the Goal Setting Scale. page 25

4. Turn to your worksheet called My Goals. Complete the My Goal Worksheet for one year, two years, and five years. page 27

   When you have completed all your work sheets, reward yourself in a way that's special to you.

   My reward to myself is _____

   _____

   _____

   _____

GOAL SETTING SCALE

Personal

_____ Things that are for me only

Mental

_____ Improve attitude
_____ Enhance intelligence
_____ Seek continuing education and training
_____ Attend workshops and seminars
_____ Purchase tapes and books
_____ Increase enthusiasm
_____ Improve self-image

GOAL SETTING WORKSHEET

THE SPECIFIC GOAL I WANT TO ACCOMPLISH IS:

_____

_____

_____

_____

THE REASONS I WANT TO REACH THIS GOAL
ARE:

_____

_____

_____

_____

THE OBSTACLES I WILL HAVE TO OVERCOME
TO REACH THIS GOAL ARE:

_____

_____

_____

_____

THE PEOPLE, GROUPS AND ORGANIZATIONS I
NEED TO WORK WITH IN ORDER TO REACH
THIS GOAL ARE:

_____

_____

_____

_____

THE KNOWLEDGE AND EDUCATION I NEED TO
REACH THIS GOAL ARE:

_____

_____

_____

_____

THE SPECIFIC PLAN OF ACTION I WILL TAKE IN
ORDER TO REACH THIS GOAL IS:

_____

_____

_____

_____

MY GOALS

My plans, where I want to be, what I want to have, and where I see myself within the next twelve months.

I.   PERSONAL

_____

_____

_____

_____

_____

_____

_____

_____

_____

_____

II.   MENTAL

_____

_____

_____

_____

_____

_____

_____

_____

_____

_____

MY GOALS

My plans, where I want to be, what I want to have, and where I see myself within the next two years.

I. PERSONAL

_____

_____

_____

_____

_____

_____

_____

_____

_____

II. MENTAL

_____

_____

_____

_____

_____

_____

_____

_____

_____

MY GOALS

My plans, where I want to be, what I want to have, and where I see myself within the next five years.

I. PERSONAL

_____

_____

_____

_____

_____

_____

_____

_____

_____

II. MENTAL

_____

_____

_____

_____

_____

_____

_____

_____

_____

Congratulations
You Have Completed Week One

WEEK TWO

Family – The family that prays together—stays together.

As we journey through life, pursuing our dreams and goals; it is important that we focus on the family. Our family members are not Barbie Dolls and GI Joes; we can't place them on a shelf and return for them when we reach our goals.

You may not have lots of time for your family; so make the time that you have quality, uninterrupted time. Praise your family members and verbally express your love for them.

> *Try to catch your family members doing something good instead of Trying to catch them doing something bad.*

This is the week to start having family meetings. Schedule them in advance; consider everyone's schedule, including the children. After all, they are people too.

Allow each member to express themselves without being judged. Remember this is a time to be heard, and not a time to be chastised for what you think and feel.

Have family members take turns expressing the good about each other. Do this each week. If you do this at the beginning of the meeting, follow the opening with a prayer; you will be amazed at how effective the outcome of even constructive criticism can be. This exercise allows each member to feel and hear something good about themselves; therefore putting them in a better frame of mind.

Look at your role as a parent and spouse. If you feel that you could have been a better parent or spouse, if you had known in the past what you know now, you are absolutely correct. So let today begin a "new day" with a "new way" of parenting and being a good partner and friend to your spouse.

> *When you learn better*
> *you*
> *Start doing better*

Do not become distraught because of the feelings your family expresses about your short-comings and neglect or abandonment, etc. This is not the week to

31

work on those feelings. Consider the discussion a "getting to know you" session.

You will learn how to resolve your family conflicts next during week three.

The following exercise will help you to understand the dynamics that promote family strength and growth.

ON YOUR MARK, READY, SET, GO!

1. Study your Goal Setting Scale. page 34

2. Turn to your worksheet called Goal Setting Worksheet. page 35

3. Complete the Goal Setting Worksheet for all items of concern from the Goal Setting Scale. page 35

4. Turn to your worksheet called My Goals. Complete the My Goal Worksheet for one year, two years, and five years. page 37

   When you have completed all your work sheets, reward yourself in a way that's special to you.

   My reward to myself is _____
   _____
   _____
   _____

GOAL SETTING SCALE

Family
_____ Improve family relationship
_____ Eat meals together
_____ Spend time together
_____ Improve listening skills
_____ Develop a forgiving attitude
_____ Be aware of tone when communicating
_____ Help, build others' self-esteem
_____ Become a good role model
_____ Become principled but flexible in disciplining
_____ Develop strategy for conflict resolution

GOAL SETTING WORKSHEET

THE SPECIFIC GOAL I WANT TO ACCOMPLISH IS:

_____

_____

_____

_____

THE REASONS I WANT TO REACH THIS GOAL ARE:

_____

_____

_____

_____

THE OBSTACLES I WILL HAVE TO OVERCOME TO REACH THIS GOAL ARE:

_____

_____

_____

_____

THE PEOPLE, GROUPS AND ORGANIZATIONS I NEED TO WORK WITH IN ORDER TO REACH THIS GOAL ARE:

_____

_____

_____

_____

THE KNOWLEDGE AND EDUCATION I NEED TO REACH THIS GOAL ARE:

_____

_____

_____

_____

THE SPECIFIC PLAN OF ACTION I WILL TAKE IN ORDER TO REACH THIS GOAL IS:

_____

_____

_____

_____

MY GOALS

My plans, where I want to be, what I want to have, and where I see myself within the next twelve months.

I. FAMILY

_____

_____

_____

_____

_____

_____

_____

_____

_____

_____

_____

_____

_____

_____

_____

_____

_____

_____

MY GOALS

My plans, where I want to be, what I want to have, and where I see myself within the next two years.

I.   FAMILY

_____

_____

_____

_____

_____

_____

_____

_____

_____

_____

_____

_____

_____

_____

_____

_____

_____

_____

_____

_____

_____

MY GOALS

My plans, where I want to be, what I want to have, and where I see myself within the next five years.

I. FAMILY

_____

_____

_____

_____

_____

_____

_____

_____

_____

_____

_____

_____

_____

_____

_____

_____

_____

_____

Congratulations
You Have Completed Week Two

WEEK THREE

Spiritual – Examine your relationship with God.

It is a good thing to study the Bible together at home. You should be the one to teach your children about spirituality. When you give them your views about God and spirituality, your children will not confuse spirituality with religion.

Openly discuss your views on the subject. Your spiritual strength is what gives you the power and endurance to weather family storms—and life's storms in general.

Your relationship with God is the most important relationship that you will ever establish.

Your spiritual beliefs are what give you the faith to overcome all obstacles and to reach for and achieve your dreams and goals.

If there is pain, hurt and un-forgiveness among you or any of your family members, this is the week to reconcile and to begin the healing process.

Have a family meeting for the purpose of healing the hurt from the past. Have each family member state any ill feelings that they are harboring against each other. Have each member ask for forgiveness, and have the person who is being asked say, "You are forgiven."

Do not get forgiveness confused with forgetting. You can forgive a person and yet have memory of the hurt they caused you. Because you openly forgave them in your heart, you can now show genuine love towards your family member.

If there is someone that you have hurt, or someone who has hurt you, and you do not feel comfortable discussing one on one, then write them a letter. Write the letter even if you are not ready to mail it. Just write it anyway. You may never mail it. It's okay. Put it in the universe to promote healing for yourself.

Now that you know who you are, that you value family, and you know where your source of strength comes from, you are now ready to move to Week 4.

ON YOUR MARK, READY, SET, GO!

1. Study your Goal Setting Scale. page 43

2. Turn to your worksheet called Goal Setting Work-sheet. page 44

3. Complete the Goal Setting Worksheet for all items of concern from the Goal Setting Scale. page 44

4. Turn to your worksheet called My Goals. Complete the My Goal Worksheet for one year, two years, and five years. page 46

   When you have completed all your work sheets, reward yourself in a way that's special to you.

   My reward to myself is _____

   _____

   _____

   _____

GOAL SETTING SCALE

Spiritual

_____ Strengthen belief in God

_____ Strive for inner peace

_____ Be a good influence on others

_____ Improve spouse relationship

_____ Become more involved in church

_____ Seek purpose for my life

_____ Improve attitude toward giving

_____ Attend Christian education classes

_____ Work on sharing with others

GOAL SETTING WORKSHEET

THE SPECIFIC GOAL I WANT TO ACCOMPLISH IS:

_____

_____

_____

_____

THE REASONS I WANT TO REACH THIS GOAL ARE:

_____

_____

_____

_____

THE OBSTACLES I WILL HAVE TO OVERCOME TO REACH THIS GOAL ARE:

_____

_____

_____

_____

THE PEOPLE, GROUPS AND ORGANIZATIONS I NEED TO WORK WITH IN ORDER TO REACH THIS GOAL ARE:

_____

_____

_____

_____

THE KNOWLEDGE AND EDUCATION I NEED TO
REACH THIS GOAL ARE:

_____

_____

_____

_____

THE SPECIFIC PLAN OF ACTION I WILL TAKE IN
ORDER TO REACH THIS GOAL IS:

_____

_____

_____

_____

MY GOALS

My plans, where I want to be, what I want to have, and where I see myself within the next twelve months.

I.   SPIRITUAL

_____

_____

_____

_____

_____

_____

_____

_____

_____

_____

_____

_____

_____

_____

_____

_____

_____

_____

_____

_____

_____

MY GOALS

My plans, where I want to be, what I want to have, and where I see myself within the next two years.

I.   SPIRITUAL

_____

_____

_____

_____

_____

_____

_____

_____

_____

_____

_____

_____

_____

_____

_____

_____

_____

_____

_____

_____

_____

MY GOALS

My plans, where I want to be, what I want to have, and where I see myself within the next five years.

I.   SPIRITUAL

_____

_____

_____

_____

_____

_____

_____

_____

_____

_____

_____

_____

_____

_____

_____

_____

_____

_____

Congratulations
You Have Completed Week Three

WEEK FOUR

Career – The work or service that you perform for pay or as a volunteer.

If you are working at a job that you do not enjoy, start making plans to seek another job. Forty-plus hours a week is too much time to spend doing something that you do not like doing.

Do not stay on a job primarily for health benefits. You can purchase insurance on your own. If you are unhappy with your work, it can impact your attitude at home.

Be aware that no job is permanent or guaranteed for life. Therefore you should always sharpen your skills and prepare yourself to be more diverse.

If you are unhappy with every job that you have had; you may want to save money and prepare to open your own business. You may want to purchase my book **"Starting A Business Made Simple."**

It is never too late to change careers or to return to school for another trade, etc. Go for your dreams as you seek purpose for your life.

This is the week that you want to take inventory of your skills and your savings accounts.

Social – Relationships with people other than your family.

Networking is vital to success. Your social skills and attitude can be beneficial for you and your family. Your family member can reap benefits from the contacts and relationships that you have established.

ON YOUR MARK, READY, SET, GO!

1. Study your Goal Setting Scale. page 52

2. Turn to your worksheet called Goal Setting Worksheet. page 53

3. Complete the Goal Setting Worksheet for all items of concern from the Goal Setting Scale. page 53

4. Turn to your worksheet called My Goals. Complete the My Goal Worksheet for one year, two years, and five years. page 55

   When you have completed all your work sheets, reward yourself in a way that's special to you.

   My reward to myself is _____
   _____
   _____
   _____

GOAL SETTING SCALE

Career

_____ Discover how I feel about what I do

_____ Understand my job

_____ Like my business

_____ Improve relationships with co-workers or employees

_____ Increase productivity

_____ Seek opportunity for job advancement

_____ Seek opportunity for business expansion

_____ Prepare for career transition

_____ Understand company goals

Social

_____ Develop self-confidence

_____ Become more at ease at gatherings

_____ Work on being friendly

_____ Be more courteous

_____ Improve listening habits

_____ Develop sense of humor

_____ Praise others

_____ Get involved in community activities

_____ Avoid gossip

_____ Be more positive

_____ Practice good personal hygiene

GOAL SETTING WORKSHEET

THE SPECIFIC GOAL I WANT TO ACCOMPLISH IS:

_____

_____

_____

_____

THE REASONS I WANT TO REACH THIS GOAL ARE:

_____

_____

_____

_____

THE OBSTACLES I WILL HAVE TO OVERCOME TO REACH THIS GOAL ARE:

_____

_____

_____

_____

THE PEOPLE, GROUPS AND ORGANIZATIONS I NEED TO WORK WITH IN ORDER TO REACH THIS GOAL ARE:

_____

_____

_____

_____

THE KNOWLEDGE AND EDUCATION I NEED TO
REACH THIS GOAL ARE:

_____

_____

_____

_____

THE SPECIFIC PLAN OF ACTION I WILL TAKE IN
ORDER TO REACH THIS GOAL IS:

_____

_____

_____

_____

MY GOALS

My plans, where I want to be, what I want to have, and where I see myself within the next twelve months.

I. CAREER

_____
_____
_____
_____
_____
_____
_____
_____
_____
_____

II. SOCIAL

_____
_____
_____
_____
_____
_____
_____
_____
_____
_____

MY GOALS

My plans, where I want to be, what I want to have, and where I see myself within the next two years.

I.   CAREER

_____

_____

_____

_____

_____

_____

_____

_____

_____

II.   SOCIAL

_____

_____

_____

_____

_____

_____

_____

_____

_____

MY GOALS

My plans, where I want to be, what I want to have, and where I see myself within the next five years.

I.   CAREER

_____

_____

_____

_____

_____

_____

_____

_____

II.   SOCIAL

_____

_____

_____

_____

_____

_____

_____

_____

Congratulations
You Have Completed Week Four

WEEK FIVE

Financial – How deep are your pockets and what do you own?

This is a good time to take inventory of your financial status, your spending, and your saving habits.

You should hold a meeting with your family to discuss family financial goals.

Have each member do a 12-month budget. Have them each make a list of the things they want during the next twelve months. Have them write down the cost, when they want it, and the order of priority.

Express the importance of living within your income and avoiding the use of credit cards.

The following is a sample budget that will help you to take inventory of your income and expenses. It will help you to know where your money is going.

ON YOUR MARK, READY, SET, GO!

MONTHLY BUDGET

Net Wages After Taxes $ _____
Other Income   _____
_____   _____
_____   _____
_____   _____

TOTAL INCOME $_____

EXPENSES:

Rent/mortgage   _____
Electrical & water co.
Gas co.   _____
Telephone   _____
    Basic charges   _____
    Charges outside of your area code   _____
    Long distance charges   _____

Groceries
    Food items   _____
    Non-food items   _____

Insurance   _____
    Life   _____
    Health (medical)   _____
    Disability   _____
    Retirement   _____
    Auto   _____
    Home   _____

Automobile   _____

    Payment or lease   _____

    Gas, oil, etc.   _____

    Maintenance   _____

Childcare   _____

Installment Payment

    Credit cards   _____

    Installment loans   _____

    Educational loans   _____

Clothing

    Purchase   _____

    Laundry   _____

    Dry cleaning   _____

Recreation & Entertainment

    Events   _____

    Dining out   _____

    Lunch at work   _____

    Vacations   _____

    Video rentals   _____

    Gyms & spas   _____

Education   _____

    Tuition   _____

    Books & tapes   _____

    Seminars   _____

Organizational
Dues   _____

Subscriptions   _____

Church
Tithes   _____

Offering   _____

Special events   _____

Uniforms, etc.   _____

Personal Care
Routine dr. visits _____

Physical   _____

Dental   _____

Hair care   _____

Nails   _____

Cosmetics   _____

Bottled Water   _____
Gardener   _____
Bus pass   _____
Children's school allowance   _____

Special Occasions   _____
Christmas gifts   _____

Birthdays   _____

Mother's Day   _____

Father's Day   _____

Bridal showers/wedding gifts   _____

Graduations   _____

Special Occasions (cont.)

Proms _____

Class ring _____

School jacket _____

Miscellaneous _____

Banquet tickets _____

Raffle tickets _____

BBQ dinners _____

Candy drives _____

Patron list _____

TOTAL EXPENSES $_____

AVERAGE/SHORTAGE $_____

Once the family budget is completed, it is not enough to just say, "here it is." Each family member must be willing to make changes. To achieve financial freedom, each family member must make a commitment to the project.

If you want conditions to change in your life, you must change. Remember, if you keep on doing what you have been doing, you will keep on getting what you have been getting. The following page is a commitment for you and your family members to complete. When each member has completed this worksheet, schedule a time to discuss each commitment.

You may want to read my book **"Getting Out of Debt Made Simple."** You will learn the importance of becoming debt free—the simple basic things that you can do to make it a reality.

COMMITMENT

"I know that if I keep on doing what I have been doing, I will keep on getting what I've been getting."

Things I will do to help cut down on expenses and to help save money.

My contributions to the project . . . . . .

1._____
2._____
3._____
4._____
5._____
6._____
7._____
8._____
9._____
10._____

Now that you have completed your budget, move forward and complete your worksheet exercises.

ON YOUR MARK, READY, SET, GO!

1. Study your Goal Setting Scale. page 66

2. Turn to your worksheet called Goal Setting Worksheet. page 67

3. Complete the Goal Setting Worksheet for all items of concern from the Goal Setting Scale. page 67

4. Turn to your worksheet called My Goals. Complete the My Goal Worksheet for one year, two years, and five years. page 69

   When you have completed all your work sheets, reward yourself in a way that's special to you.

   My reward to myself is _____

   _____

   _____

   _____

GOAL SETTING SCALE

Financial

____ Evaluate earnings
____ Live within income
____ Set a personal budget
____ Place proper priority
____ Increase savings
____ Prepare financial statement
____ Make investments
____ Stop excessive impulse purchasing
____ Cease using charge accounts
____ Assess insurance needs

GOAL SETTING WORKSHEET

THE SPECIFIC GOAL I WANT TO ACCOMPLISH IS:

_____

_____

_____

_____

THE REASONS I WANT TO REACH THIS GOAL ARE:

_____

_____

_____

_____

THE OBSTACLES I WILL HAVE TO OVERCOME TO REACH THIS GOAL ARE:

_____

_____

_____

_____

THE PEOPLE, GROUPS AND ORGANIZATIONS I NEED TO WORK WITH IN ORDER TO REACH THIS GOAL ARE:

_____

_____

_____

_____

THE KNOWLEDGE AND EDUCATION I NEED TO
REACH THIS GOAL ARE:

_____

_____

_____

_____

THE SPECIFIC PLAN OF ACTION I WILL TAKE IN
ORDER TO REACH THIS GOAL IS:

_____

_____

_____

_____

MY GOALS

My plans, where I want to be, what I want to have, and where I see myself within the next twelve months.

I.   FINANCIAL

_____

_____

_____

_____

_____

_____

_____

_____

_____

_____

_____

_____

_____

_____

_____

_____

_____

_____

_____

MY GOALS

My plans, where I want to be, what I want to have, and where I see myself within the next two years.

I.   FINANCIAL

_____
_____
_____
_____
_____
_____
_____
_____
_____
_____
_____
_____
_____
_____
_____
_____
_____
_____
_____

MY GOALS

My plans, where I want to be, what I want to have, and where I see myself within the next five years.

I.   FINANCIAL

_____

_____

_____

_____

_____

_____

_____

_____

_____

_____

_____

_____

_____

_____

_____

_____

_____

_____

Congratulations
You Have Completed Week Five

WEEK SIX

Physical – Your state of health—condition of your physical body.

Good health is important. When we have good health, we have more energy and vitality and therefore we are better at all that we do.

Stop now and take inventory of your health status.

1. Are you satisfied with how you feel
    most of the time?   _____
2. Are you satisfied with your weight?   _____
3. Are you satisfied with your diet?   _____
4. Are you satisfied with how
    your children eat?   _____
5. Are you willing to change your eating
    habits so that you can experience
    better health?   _____

There are many books on the market that lend themselves to helping you make better decisions about your health choices. Visit your local bookstore.

This is the week to start a new trend for your family.

You and your family will never forget the experience that this week will bring if you do the following:

- Prepare breakfast at home every day this week.
- Insure every family member sits at the same table and eats.
- Offer prayer by a different family member each day.
- Prepare lunch at home each day.
- Prepare dinner at home each day.

The habits that you have developed during these six weeks will, without a doubt, change your life forever.

You are now ready to complete the last worksheets. I hope that this journey has put you on the path to creating a "New You."

Sexual – When it comes to sex, the first thing we must understand is that having sex with someone does not mean that you love that person. And feeling love for someone does not mean that you want to have sex with that person.

As we have discussed earlier, making changes can bring about turbulence in your life, but this too shall pass. You should not see sex as a means to develop love between two people; instead, love should be developed between two people before they think of having sex. Sex is a communion between two people that enhances love and promotes bonding. When sex becomes a recreational activity for you, then you are heading for disaster and much turbulence in your life.

O.K., I have your questions. You want to start all over again with your sexual life and not have sex at all until you are married, or at least until your partner and you are discussing love and marriage. But how do you stop having sex with your partner?

Well, you simply talk to your partner about the changes that you are making in your life and discuss the new direction you are taking in your sexual life. Let him/her know that the change has nothing to do with your love for him/her, but the change is all about your journey of creating a new perspective for yourself.

O.K., I hear you. You said, how can you tell your partner that you are not sexually active when you already have a child?

Well, understand that our past is the past. Explain to your partner that there are sexual decisions that you made in the past that were not good for you. Therefore, you are carving a new path for yourself that will be more mentally and emotionally healthy for you and your child. Tell him/her that you love him/her very much; however, you have made a choice to not have sex outside of marriage. And let the chips fall where they may. Some choices that you will have to make are personal choices. Make them.

Food for thought for your sexual fulfillment.

> *Stroke the mind*
> *Before the behind*

> *If you don't know what you want*
> *sexually you will*
> *never have your sexual needs met*

> *If you do not tell your partner*
> *what you want in bed*
> *you will*
> *get what his other bed*
> *partner wanted in bed*

> *Always make your sexual agenda*
> *understood*
> *and yes a quickie is ok.*
> *But, don't have your partner*
> *preparing for a long trip,*
> *if you are just going around the corner*

> *Sexual empowerment is*
> *not how well some one else*
> *can please you, but*
> *how well you can please*
> *yourself sexually*

Closing thought on creating a new you and becoming the person you want to become sexually.

- If sexual intercourse is not of interest to you, don't engage.
- If having sex has been a way of proving your love for your mate—find another way.
- Sex should not provoke physical or emotional pain.
- Explore your own body and discover what turns you on.
- Do not be afraid or ashamed to guide your mate to the right spot and position that gives you the most pleasure. After all, this should be someone who cares about pleasing you.
- Discuss hygiene openly when it interferes with intimacy.
- Sex should not provoke physical or emotional pain.
- Discuss hygiene openly when it interferes with intimacy.

- If you are married, take time for your sexual excursion. Sex should not be a mere duty or chore for you.
- If you have sexual challenges due to past experiences in your life, seek professional help.

If sex is the vehicle that you have used to get what you want, find another way to accomplish the same goal; you will feel better about both yourself and sex.

Now that you have explored your sexuality and your sexual appetite, you should feel comfortable doing the following exercises.

ON YOUR MARK, READY, SET, GO!

1. Study your Goal Setting Scale. page 80

2. Turn to your worksheet called Goal Setting Worksheet. page 81

3. Complete the Goal Setting Worksheet for all items of concern from the Goal Setting Scale. page 81

4. Turn to your worksheet called My Goals. Complete the My Goal Worksheet for one year, two years, and five years. page 83

   When you have completed all your work sheets, reward yourself in a way that's special to you.

   My reward to myself is _____
   _____
   _____
   _____

GOAL SETTING SCALE

Physical

_____ Improve appearance
_____ Assess energy level
_____ Plan recreational activities
_____ Participate in regular fitness program
_____ Schedule regular medical and dental checkups
_____ Manage stress control
_____ Plan a healthy diet and nutrition program
_____ Manage weight control

Sexual

_____ Explore my body
_____ Express my sexual needs
_____ Share past experiences that are not conductive to good sex with my partner
_____ Find ways to get what I want from my mate without the use of sex
_____ Have courage to demand having protected sex only
_____ Openly discuss personal hygiene with my mate
_____ Make more time for intimacy with mate
_____ Initiate sexual intercourse
_____ Say no to sex and mean no

GOAL SETTING WORKSHEET

THE SPECIFIC GOAL I WANT TO ACCOMPLISH IS:

_____

_____

_____

_____

THE REASONS I WANT TO REACH THIS GOAL ARE:

_____

_____

_____

_____

THE OBSTACLES I WILL HAVE TO OVERCOME TO REACH THIS GOAL ARE:

_____

_____

_____

_____

THE PEOPLE, GROUPS AND ORGANIZATIONS I NEED TO WORK WITH IN ORDER TO REACH THIS GOAL ARE:

_____

_____

_____

_____

THE KNOWLEDGE AND EDUCATION I NEED TO REACH THIS GOAL ARE:

_____

_____

_____

_____

THE SPECIFIC PLAN OF ACTION I WILL TAKE IN ORDER TO REACH THIS GOAL IS:

_____

_____

_____

_____

MY GOALS

My plans, where I want to be, what I want to have, and where I see myself within the next twelve months.

I.   PHYSICAL

_____

_____

_____

_____

_____

_____

_____

_____

_____

_____

II.   SEXUAL

_____

_____

_____

_____

_____

_____

_____

_____

_____

_____

MY GOALS

My plans, where I want to be, what I want to have, and where I see myself within the next two years.

I. PHYSICAL

_____

_____

_____

_____

_____

_____

_____

_____

II. SEXUAL

_____

_____

_____

_____

_____

_____

_____

_____

MY GOALS

My plans, where I want to be, what I want to have, and where I see myself within the next five years.

I. PHYSICAL

_____

_____

_____

_____

_____

_____

_____

_____

_____

_____

II. SEXUAL

_____

_____

_____

_____

_____

_____

_____

_____

_____

_____

CONCLUSION –

I am sure by now you have the recipe to bake this cake called "change," creating a new you. What did you say? Did you say it's not easy? I never alluded to the fact that it would be easy. The only promise I made to you, was that it is possible.

Let's look at the ingredients needed. First you need a large desire bowl to mix the ingredients.

- Pour in 10 cups of courage, you need enough courage to soak up all your other ingredients.
- Add 5 cups of persistence—the persistence helps to make the stirring easier when mixing the other ingredients.
- Add 5 cups of consistency, then bring to a boil for 30 minutes. Then let it cool before adding your last ingredient—perseverance.
- Consistency removes all lumps from the substance and makes it smooth.
- Now add 10 cups of Perseverance, this is your final step. Stir the perseverance until substance becomes firm. Then layer with large amounts of love, and faith, and let set in the refrigerator until ready to be eaten.

When you begin to make a change in your life, you will feel like you are, being eaten alive. So you've got to be firm and ready for the revolution. It can be a difficult battle, so be prepared. A great book to read is, *"Who Moved My Cheese,"* by Spencer Johnson, M.D.

Let's look at things you will encounter during your "new you" transformation.

You will get much resistance from your partner, family members, friends and co-workers. Why? Because they are accustomed to your being predictable and now you are becoming unpredictable. Your changing is forcing those whom you have relationships with to make changes also, because:

- you are saying no sometimes instead of always saying yes.
- you are putting yourself first instead of others first.
- you are no longer doing their work for them.
- you are now speaking up for yourself.
- you are telling people exactly what you think and feel.
- you are no longer the doormat for everybody to walk over.
- you are feeling like the head and not the tail.
- you are no longer going along to get along.
- you are demanding respect from others.

- you are letting people know when they hurt you.
- you are demanding your money from others when you have made them a loan (suing, pursuing, and taking them to court).
- you are expressing your likes and dislikes with your sexual partner.
- you are now telling your mate what it is that you need for sexual fulfillment.
- you are initiating sexual intercourse and not feeling guilty.
- you will not have unsafe, unprotected sex.

Now you should be better able to understand the significance of the recipe you read earlier. These are the ingredients necessary to bring you to self-empowerment status in every aspect of your life.

It is important to have balance in your life. You must empower yourself in every aspect when seeking to transform your life. It is vital to take personal and mental inventory. How you see and feel about self and your mental status will determine how you will deal with your family, your spirituality, your career and social life, your financial status, your physical self and your sexuality.

It is important to bring balance in all these areas. For example, when you do not feel good about your appearance, it can impact your self-esteem, therefore; affecting your social life as well as, in your career. This will affect upward mobility, financial status, and life style for yourself and that of your family.

For these reasons, it is important for you to complete this book in the order of its presentation, beginning with the introduction.

This book is designed to help readers to achieve their personal quest for happiness and fulfillment; and the courage to pursue their own agenda without feeling guilty.

Congratulations!
Now celebrate the
new person that you have become.

You have
my permission
to change!

JUST
DO
IT!

Homework Assignment
Describe the "New You."

Personally

_____

_____

_____

_____

_____

_____

_____

_____

_____

_____

_____

_____

_____

Rate your growth on the scale of 1 to 10, 10 being the highest
(Circle the number that shows your growth)

1 2 3 4 5 6 7 8 9 10

What did you say? You fell down, you fell short, so what!

> *It's not how many times*
> *we fall down that counts.*
> *It's how often we get back up.*

Homework Assignment
Describe the "New You."

Mentally

_____

_____

_____

_____

_____

_____

_____

_____

_____

_____

_____

_____

Rate your growth on the scale of 1 to 10, 10 being the highest
(Circle the number that shows your growth)

1 2 3 4 5 6 7 8 9 10

What did you say? You fell down, you fell short, so what!

> *It's not how many times*
> *we fall down that counts.*
> *It's how often we get back up.*

Homework Assignment
Describe the "New You."

Spiritually

_____

_____

_____

_____

_____

_____

_____

_____

_____

_____

_____

_____

_____

Rate your growth on the scale of 1 to 10, 10 being the highest
(Circle the number that shows your growth)

1 2 3 4 5 6 7 8 9 10

What did you say? You fell down, you fell short, so what!

> *It's not how many times*
> *we fall down that counts.*
> *It's how often we get back up.*

Homework Assignment
Describe the "New You."

Socially

_____

_____

_____

_____

_____

_____

_____

_____

_____

_____

_____

_____

_____

Rate your growth on the scale of 1 to 10, 10 being the highest
(Circle the number that shows your growth)

1 2 3 4 5 6 7 8 9 10

What did you say? You fell down, you fell short, so what!

> *It's not how many times*
> *we fall down that counts.*
> *It's how often we get back up.*

Homework Assignment
Describe the "New You."

Physically

_____

_____

_____

_____

_____

_____

_____

_____

_____

_____

_____

_____

_____

Rate your growth on the scale of 1 to 10, 10 being the highest
(Circle the number that shows your growth)

1 2 3 4 5 6 7 8 9 10

What did you say? You fell down, you fell short, so what!

> *It's not how many times*
> *we fall down that counts.*
> *It's how often we get back up.*

Homework Assignment
Describe the "New You."

Financially

_____

_____

_____

_____

_____

_____

_____

_____

_____

_____

_____

_____

Rate your growth on the scale of 1 to 10, 10 being the highest
(Circle the number that shows your growth)

1 2 3 4 5 6 7 8 9 10

What did you say? You fell down, you fell short, so what!

> *It's not how many times*
> *we fall down that counts.*
> *It's how often we get back up.*

Homework Assignment
Describe the "New You."

Sexually

_____

_____

_____

_____

_____

_____

_____

_____

_____

_____

_____

_____

_____

Rate your growth on the scale of 1 to 10, 10 being the highest
(Circle the number that shows your growth)

1 2 3 4 5 6 7 8 9 10

What did you say? You fell down, you fell short, so what!

> *It's not how many times*
> *we fall down that counts.*
> *It's how often we get back up.*

Homework Assignment
Describe the "New You."

Family Life

_____

_____

_____

_____

_____

_____

_____

_____

_____

_____

_____

_____

_____

Rate your growth on the scale of 1 to 10, 10 being the highest
(Circle the number that shows your growth)

1 2 3 4 5 6 7 8 9 10

What did you say? You fell down, you fell short, so what!

> *It's not how many times
> we fall down that counts.
> It's how often we get back up.*

Homework Assignment
Describe the "New You."

My Career

_____

_____

_____

_____

_____

_____

_____

_____

_____

_____

_____

_____

Rate your growth on the scale of 1 to 10, 10 being the highest
(Circle the number that shows your growth)

1 2 3 4 5 6 7 8 9 10

What did you say? You fell down, you fell short, so what!

> *It's not how many times*
> *we fall down that counts.*
> *It's how often we get back up.*

Special Notes

_____

_____

_____

_____

_____

_____

_____

_____

_____

_____

_____

_____

_____

_____

_____

_____

_____

What did you say? You fell down, you fell short, so what!

> *It's not how many times*
> *we fall down that counts.*
> *It's how often we get back up.*

BOOK AVAILABLE THROUGH
Milligan Books, Inc.
An Imprint Of Professional Business
Consulting Service

Creating A New You In Six Weeks $13.00

Order Form

Milligan Books
1425 West Manchester, Suite B,
Los Angeles, California 90047
(323) 750-3592

Mail Check or Money Order to:
Milligan Books

Name _____ Date _____

Address _____

City_____ State ____ Zip Code_____

Day telephone _____

Evening telephone_____

Book title _____

Number of books ordered ___ Total cost .... $ _____

Sales Taxes (CA Add 8.25%)............................... $ _____

Shipping & Handling $4.50 per book.....................$ _____

Total Amount Due... $ _____

_ Check   _ Money Order   Other Cards _____

_ Visa   _ Master Card   Expiration Date _____

Credit Card No. _____

Driver's License No. _____

Signature _____   Date _____

www.ingramcontent.com/pod-product-compliance
Lightning Source LLC
LaVergne TN
LVHW011409080426
835511LV00005B/446